C. Hubert H.

Parry

Songs of Farewell

Edited by Robert Quinney

vocal score

MUSIC DEPARTMENT

OXFORD
UNIVERSITY PRESS

OXFORD
UNIVERSITY PRESS

Great Clarendon Street, Oxford OX2 6DP,
United Kingdom

Oxford University Press is a department of the University of Oxford.
It furthers the University's objective of excellence in research, scholarship,
and education by publishing worldwide. Oxford is a registered trade mark of
Oxford University Press in the UK and in certain other countries

First published 2017

Impression: 4

ISBN 978–0–19–351846–9

Music origination by Andrew Jones
Text origination by Michael Durnin
Printed in Great Britain on acid-free paper by
Halstan & Co. Ltd, Amersham, Bucks.

PREFACE

Charles Hubert Hastings Parry was a dominant force in British music-making in the four decades between the premiere of *Prometheus Unbound* in 1879 and his death in October 1918. His music, with that of his contemporary Charles Villiers Stanford, brought the music of his native land into the European mainstream, through its assimilation of continental—specifically German—models. His activity as a pedagogue, principally as Director of the Royal College of Music from 1895, greatly influenced a generation of British musicians that included Vaughan Williams, Holst, Howells, Bliss, and Finzi.

Parry is now best known for his coronation anthem *I was glad when they said unto me* and unison setting of Blake's *Jerusalem*: works whose ceremonial-cum-nationalistic associations give an incomplete picture of a composer who was also capable of a deeply affecting introspection. The late set of motets, *Songs of Farewell*, are among his greatest achievements, and have found a secure place in the repertoires of chamber choirs and ecclesiastical choral foundations. While not all are devotional, the texts meditate upon the transience of life, and some are explicitly valedictory in tone—most notably the last of the six, a setting of the greater portion of Psalm 39 (and thus the only piece of scripture in the set), *Lord, let me know mine end*.

It is clear that Parry had not settled an order for the motets as he composed them, though manuscripts include superscriptions such as 'for the group called *Songs of Farewell*'. The first motet is labelled 'No 4' in the latest of the autographs, and the first to be composed was in fact the fourth, *There is an old belief*, which was performed in its original version at the Royal Mausoleum at Frogmore in January 1907. In 1913 it was revised, and at this point Parry began to assemble a set around it: first *Never weather-beaten sail*, then *I know my soul hath power*, and, in an apparently tortuous process of drafting and redrafting, *My soul, there is a country*. (The final form of *There is an old belief* seems not to have been reached until shortly before publication in 1916.) Towards the end of 1915 he completed the set with *At the round earth's imagined corners* and *Lord, let me know mine end*.

The technical accomplishments of the *Songs of Farewell* are considerable. The influence of choral music by Mendelssohn and Brahms is very much in evidence: the control of texture in up to eight voices, perhaps most effective in the sinuous contrapuntal lines of the fifth, and the virtuosic double-choir writing of the sixth motet; the exquisitely balanced alternation between simple and compound time in *My soul, there is a country*; and the syllabic directness of *I know my soul hath power* and *There is an old belief*.

The context provided by both the Great War and Parry's declining health (he was suffering from heart failure, sometimes sustaining several small 'heart attacks' in the course of a week by the mid-1910s) adds great poignancy to the motets. The war had disastrous significance for Parry in two ways. First, it signalled a bitter end to decades of cultural cross-fertilization between Britain and Germany; this had influenced not only Parry's own education (through his studies in Stuttgart, and in London with the German-educated pianist Edward Dannreuther, which brought him into contact with Wagner among others), but also his professional life at the Royal College of Music, which had been founded in 1882 on the German *Hochschule* model. Secondly, it robbed the country of many talented young musicians known to Parry, including two alumni of the RCM: George Butterworth, who died at the Somme in 1916, and Ernest Farrar, whose death preceded Parry's own by less than a month. It is difficult to hear the passage 'and you whose eyes shall behold God' in *At the round earth's imagined corners* without thinking of the sacrifice of these young men—even though its composition predates the death of Butterworth and Farrar. Likewise, the closing section of *Lord, let me know mine end* seems inextricably linked to the composer's physical decline: 'O spare me a little, that I may recover my strength, before I go hence, and be no more seen'. Parry died on 7 October 1918, just over a month before the Armistice; he had heard all six motets performed separately, and the first five together in May 1916, but they were only given as a complete set on 23 February 1919, at a memorial concert in Exeter College Chapel, Oxford, sung by the choirs of New College and Christ Church together with members of the Oxford Bach Choir, under Hugh Allen.

ROBERT QUINNEY
New College, Oxford, 2017

TEXTUAL NOTES

Editorial practice

As with other editions in the *Classic Choral Works* series, the aim is first and foremost to serve the practical needs of choirs, keeping the music pages as clean and uncluttered as possible, though not neglecting the needs of the scholar. To that end I have not noted changes and corrections in the text, but have instead listed them in the Variants. Beaming has been modernized, and the keyboard reduction aims to be playable, rather than representing every voice, with voice-leading lines mostly omitted for the sake of legibility. In places where the outer notes of the choral texture exceed a hand span, cue-sized notes have been employed at one extremity; the player may omit these, or spread the chord.

The complete autograph copies (as opposed to sketches) of the motets were clearly not the final stage in the compositional process. There are several variants from the first editions, presumably corrected on proofs. A set of handwritten printed versions (**B** in the source list below) almost invariably follow the complete autographs, so it seems likely that Parry made changes following performances for which these early prints were used. (The early printed version of *Lord, let me know mine end* is bound into a choirbook of anthems in New College Library; it seems the college did not own the 1918 published version until the Cramer reprint was purchased in 1995.)

The several variants notwithstanding, in matters such as the placing of dynamic hairpins I have often preferred the autograph manuscripts: the beginning and end points of the hairpin follows Parry's hand as closely as is possible or practicable, except where an illogical placing can be explained by lack of space. For the most part Parry is remarkably specific in his placing of hairpins, though it must be admitted that he clearly did not correct publication proofs so as more accurately to reflect his notation—perhaps because printing technology did not allow for greater precision. The autograph manuscripts are, however, inconsistent in their use of '*cresc.*' vs hairpins: e.g. the opening phrase of *Never weather-beaten sail* gives '*cresc.*' in Soprano 1 and Bass, a hairpin in Tenor, and nothing in the remaining voices. Here and in comparable places I have preferred hairpins, except where *cresc.* appears to denote longer-term dynamic change (*see* 'Performance considerations'). The first editions of motets 1 to 4 were furnished with metronome marks; editorial suggestions have been made in the remaining two motets, both of which feature several changes of tempo.

Parry is liberal in his use of articulation marks, which are often employed inconsistently between voices carrying the same material in imitation: e.g. *At the round earth's imagined corners*, b. 55, between Alto 1 and Bass 1, and the inconsistent use of staccato dots on 'sleep' elsewhere in this section. I have never deleted a marking made by Parry unless it seems entirely inconsistent and therefore potentially accidental. Neither have I always extrapolated articulation or dynamic markings from one voice to others, in part to preserve as clearly legible a score as possible; the first edition generally extrapolates more than the present edition, sometimes incorrectly to my mind. Where inconsistency occurs, it may of course be corrected by performers. Throughout, Parry's notational habit of tying a crotchet to a succeeding quaver in preference to writing a dotted crotchet has been retained, as in the first edition.

The autographs suggest that Parry composed at least some of the set to memorized texts, judging by the high frequency of errors: e.g. the third motet opens 'Never weatherbeaten *ship* more willing bent to shore, Never *wearied* pilgrims' limbs ... ', and the fifth has 'here in lowly ground' miscorrected to 'here on this holy ground'. Some apparent errors may reflect the edition from which Parry had learnt his texts; the transposition of 'she is' to 'is she' in the second motet appears also in the edition of Sir John Davies' poetry by Alexander Balloch Grosart (1876), which may therefore be Parry's source.

The version of *There is an old belief* transmitted in **B**, which may be the closest complete source to the 1907 original, is available for download from the Companion Website: www.oup.com/songsoffarewell.

Sources and variants

A **Oxford, Bodleian Library, MS. Mus. c.127**
Several autograph manuscripts, including many drafts of the six motets 'Songs of Farewell'. The most complete drafts were apparently used by printers for **B** and **C** below. These appear on fols 1–220, occupying most of the book.

B **Oxford, Bodleian Library, Mus. 2016 d.2**
Formerly in the Oxford Music Faculty library. These individual copies of the motets appear to have been handwritten and reproduced for pre-publication performances, including those by New College Choir. With the exception of hairpin placement, these faithfully reproduce the text of **A**; certain changes were made (on proof copies now lost?) between the production of **B** and publication of **C**, perhaps following early performances.

C **First editions**
Motets 1–4: The Year Book Press, 1916
Motet 5: The Year Book Press, 1917
Motet 6: H.F.W. Deane, 1918
The motets were issued separately, though all identified as 'for the group called "Songs of Farewell"'; a complete reprint was issued by Cramer Music in 1989.

The new edition is based largely upon **C**, the final text, but with several changes to notational details. These have been made with reference to **A** and **B**, and are detailed below.

1. My soul, there is a country

b. 1: tempo indication 'Slow': **A** & **B** give 'Moderate'

b. 19: in place of the fermata **A** & **B** set 'files' to ♩., tied across the double barline to ♩ in b. 20

b. 25: in **A**, accent on Alto 'love', included here (in **B** & **C**, no accent)

b. 30: no tempo indication in **A** or **B**

b. 41, Tenor: first note C in **A** & **B**

b. 46, Soprano: final note E in most versions in **A** & **B**. Parry is undecided whether to continue the Tenor phrase up to G, which requires a final G in the Soprano to avoid consecutive octaves, or send it to D via C; in the end he opts to retain imitation in the Tenor, while preferring the bolder octave leap in the Soprano (avoiding a less obvious pair of consecutives in the process)

b. 60: *allargando* in **C** only

b. 62: the accent on 'One' does not appear in **C** or **B**; it was added to the complete version of the motet in **A** in pencil, but seems to have been missed by the copyist

2. I know my soul hath power to know all things

b. 3: in **A**, staccato dot above final ♪ (in Soprano only)

b. 4: in **A**, text (underlaid to Soprano and Tenor throughout) 'Yet is she'

bb. 11–12: in **A**, text 'I'm thrall'

bb. 20–5: the three sources differ in various ways. In b. 20 **C** follows **A**, while **B** moves to A♭ major (a modulation found in none of the sketches bound in **A**, suggesting the existence of another draft, now lost); the final version of bb. 21–5 is an amalgam of **A** & **B**.

3. Never weather-beaten sail

b. 1, Soprano 1: in **A**, first note is E; in **B**, the printed E is corrected in pencil to a C below, bringing it into line with **C**

b. 5: in **A**, *'espress.'* is written above Soprano 1 only; I take this marking to refer to the accented dissonance in the two highest voices only

bb. 12–14, Soprano 1: in **A** & **B**, ⟨ begins earlier, and ⟩ begins later than in **C**; this placement has been adopted

b. 31, Soprano 1: in **A** & **B**, crotchet G on 'ev-'; corrected in pencil to E in print

bb. 35–6, Soprano 1: *p* dynamic above 'age', not 'cold' in **A** & **B**

b. 39, Soprano 2: in **A** & **B**, ⟨ begins at the start of the phrase, not in b. 40 as in **C**

b. 42, Bass: in **A** & **B**, ⟨ above 'sun'

bb. 51–2: in **A** & **B**, *p* dynamic above Bass and Alto only; in **C**, above Bass only

b. 54, Soprano 2: no hairpin in **A** or **B**, but cf. b. 22

b. 55, Bass: no ⟩ in **A** or **B**

b. 56: in **A** & **B**, no ⟩ in Alto or Tenor, but these have been extrapolated from Soprano 1 and Bass

b. 58: placement of *allargando* in **A** & **B** preferred

b. 59, Tenor: **A** & **B** give dynamic *mf*, not *f* as in **C**

b. 61: in **A** & **B**, no ⟩

4. There is an old belief

C represents a different version of the motet from that transmitted by **B** and by most of the five incomplete drafts in **A**. The chronology is unclear, but it seems likely that **A** & **B** include passages from the first version, performed in 1907. **B** follows, almost exactly, the first draft in **A** (though this lacks the first four bars). The final form of the opening does not appear in any source but **C**, and the final form of the section 'serene in changeless prime of body and of soul' appears only in the fourth of the five drafts in **A**.

b. 4, Soprano 2: *p* dynamic moved in this edition to the first syllable of the phrase

5. At the round earth's imagined corners

All sources lack a metronome mark; editorial suggestions have been made at all tempo changes in the motet.

b. 1, Alto 2 & Bass 2: hairpin placement in **A** preferred

b. 4, Tenor: accent, present in **A** but missing from **B** & **C**, reinstated

b. 5: *cresc.* marking in all sources removed; this duplicates the instruction in b. 4. It may have been written because there is a page break in **A** between bb. 4 and 5.

b. 12, Alto 2: ⟨, in **C** but not **A** or **B**, removed. Note the downward trajectory of the phrase.

bb. 13–14, Soprano 1 & Bass 1: two hairpins in successive bars combined. There is a page break in **A** between the two bars.

b. 17: in **A**, *'cresc.'* written above third beat of bar, followed by a horizontal line reaching to the *mf* entry of Soprano 1 in b. 19, suggesting Parry conceived of a gradual crescendo between these points, not a sudden increase at voice entries marked *mf* (*see* note on Parry's use of *mf* in 'Performance considerations')

b. 17, Alto 1: ⟨, present in **A** & **B** but missing from **C**, reinstated

b. 19, Tenor: accent missing in **B** & **C**, present in **A**, on second syllable of 'infinities'

b. 22, Alto 1: hairpin placement in **A** & **B** preferred

b. 23, Soprano 2: I have preferred the ⟩ in **A** to the *dim.* marking in **B** & **C**

bb. 26, 28: in **A**, the word 'flood' has a staccato dot in Tenor (b. 26) and in all voices but Alto 2 (b. 28); these are not found in **B** or **C**, but have been reinstated

b. 28: in **A** & **B** the dotted rhythm is absent, and 'the' is omitted from the text

bb. 29–30, Soprano 2: accents added to match Soprano 1; all sources have an accent on 'shall' only

b. 30, Soprano 2: accent added to match Soprano 1

b. 30, Bass 2: accents on final two notes missing in all sources, instated to be consistent with Bass 1

b. 37, Soprano 2: in **C**, perhaps because of line break, ‿‿‿ does not continue into b. 38 as in **A** & **B**; hairpin extended to end of 'behold' as in **A**

b. 41, Soprano 2: hairpin placement in **A** preferred to that in **B** & **C**

b. 46: in **A**, Alto 1 has hairpin as well as Soprano 2. I have reinstated this in Alto 1 and applied it to Alto 2 as well, since the implication seems to be of an expressive shape to the first syllable of 'never', within the context of a general *diminuendo*

b. 51: **A** gives tempo indication 'Very slow', replacing crossed-out 'Adagiosissimo' (*sic*); **B** has no tempo change at this point

b. 53, Alto 2: in **A**, ⟨ begins later; this reading preferred

b. 71: in **A**, *poco rit.* begins on third beat of bar; placement in **B** & **C** preferred

bb. 77–8, Alto 1 & 2: in **A**, Alto 1 has the second (*diminuendo*) half of the hairpin in Soprano 1 and 2. I have included this, extending the hairpin shape to all four upper voices, to match the *crescendo* in the lower three voices that follows

bb. 81–2, Tenor, Bass 1 & 2: hairpin placement in **A** preferred

bb. 89–90, Soprano 1 & 2: hairpin placement in **A** preferred

b. 90, Soprano 2: accent in **A** reinstated

bb. 92–3, Soprano 2: ⟩ in **A** reinstated

6. Lord, let me know mine end

All sources lack a metronome mark; editorial suggestions have been made at all tempo changes in the motet.

bb. 13–14: ⟨, broken by page break in **A** and reproduced thus in **B** & **C**, unified to cover both bars

b. 30: Soprano and Alto in both choirs have a redundant ***pp*** marking, possibly because of a page turn before this bar in **A**; this has been deleted

b. 36: in **A**, the ⟩ in the upper four voices is reproduced only in Ch. 1 Tenor; **B** extrapolates this to both Bass parts, and **C** to all voices. I have removed the hairpin from Ch. 1 Tenor, suspecting this to be an error, and it therefore does not appear in any of the lower voices.

b. 36, Ch. 2 Soprano: accent added to match Ch. 1 Soprano

b. 49: in **A** & **B** there is no ⟨ in any voice until b. 50. These are present in every voice in **C**, but since they are somewhat counterintuitive they have been omitted here.

b. 52: in **A** the tempo indication *Allegro* is accompanied by a leftward-pointing arrow, presumably written later, which suggests the new tempo begin halfway through b. 51. This reading appears in **B**, but not in **C**; the later (and also presumably original) version seems preferable, since it allows for a tempo modulation that renders the final note of b. 51 equal to its imitation in b. 53.

b. 72, Ch. 1 Bass: ⟨ in **A** & **B** reinstated

b. 74, Ch. 2 Tenor: ⟨ in **A** reinstated

b. 76, Ch. 1 Soprano: accent on 'means' in **C** but not **A** or **B**. Since there is no accent on this syllable elsewhere in the section I have deleted it.

bb. 76–7, Ch. 2 Tenor: hairpin, present in **A** but not **B** or **C**, reinstated

bb. 89–90, Ch. 2 Tenor: ⟩ in **A** reinstated

bb. 90–1, Ch. 1 Tenor: later ⟩ in **A** preferred

bb. 96–9: hairpin placement in **A** preferred

bb. 101, 103: *dim.* placement in **A** preferred

bb. 107–9: dynamic marking placement in **A** preferred

b. 112, Ch. 2 Bass: accent in **A** and early print reinstated

b. 115, Ch. 2: hairpin placement in **A** preferred

b. 119, Ch. 1 Alto and b. 121, Ch. 1 Soprano: accent on 'thee', present in **C** but absent in **A** & **B**, deleted

b. 124, Ch. 2 Soprano: accent in **A** reinstated

b. 125, Ch. 1 Bass: ⟩, absent from **A** & **B**, deleted

b. 129, Ch. 1 Soprano: accent in **A** reinstated

bb. 130–1, Ch. 1 Soprano: hairpin placement in **A** preferred

b. 131, Ch. 1 Alto and Bass: hairpins, absent from **A** & **B**, deleted

bb. 136–7, Ch. 1 Alto: hairpins, absent from **A** & **B**, deleted

b. 139–end: all hairpin placements in **A** preferred

Performance considerations

Tempo and metric modulation

The metronome marks provided for the first four motets appear in **C** only. The final two motets, which are also the longest and most sectional, have no metronome marks; I have provided suggestions in square brackets. Parry never specifies a proportional relationship between successive tempi, but there are transitions in the first and last of the motets where a strict relationship is effective, and may even have been intended:

My soul, there is a country, bb. 38–9, if the ♪ remains constant, b. 38 may be given in hemiola, i.e. divided into three groups of two ♪s, with 'ease' occupying a ♩ in the new time signature. The marking 'Animato' may be taken to indicate a slight quickening of the pulse in b. 39.

Lord, let me know mine end: bb. 51–2, if ♪ becomes ♩, the upbeat 'de-' sung by Choir 2 is of equal length to that sung by Choir 1 at the end of b. 53.

Dynamics and articulation

Parry never uses the dynamic ***mp***; performers must therefore exercise discretion in their interpretation of the marking ***mf***, which is the only dynamic gradation between ***p*** and ***f***. In general, Parry seems to use hairpin markings for 'local' dynamic change, i.e. affecting the notes covered by the hairpin; *cresc.* and *dim.* should be read as denoting longer-term change, and taken to apply until countermanded by another dynamic marking. For example, see *Lord, let me know mine end*, bb. 107f: *dim.* may be taken to apply to the whole phrase up to the general bar's rest, with hairpins showing an up–down dynamic shaping in the Alto and Bass voices.

Parry makes liberal use of accents [>] throughout the six motets. In many places these appear to denote not a sharp attack, but rather a point of particular focus in the phrase, often in tandem with a dissonance (e.g. *There is an old belief*, b. 2, Soprano 2 and Bass 1). With this in mind, I have in some places extrapolated accents from one voice to another, and elsewhere I have removed accents that seem incorrectly to have been applied by an earlier engraver or editor.

Rescoring

Choirs in which the alto line is sung by countertenors may find the following rescored passages from *At the round earth's imagined corners* helpful, in which the tessitura has an upper limit of d'''. In *Lord, let me know mine end* the Choir 2 Alto f'' at b. 83 may be avoided by swapping the Choir 2 Soprano and Alto entries, and the Altos ending the phrase an octave lower than notated in b. 84.

1. *At the round earth's imagined corners*, bars 5–11, soprano and alto parts.

2. *At the round earth's imagined corners*, bars 56–60, soprano and alto parts.

Full-sized versions of these examples for use in performance are available for download from the Companion Website: www.oup.com/songsoffarewell.

Performance style

The *Songs of Farewell* owe much of their intimate character to the secular part-song, of which Parry was perhaps the leading exponent in the late Victorian/Edwardian period. They are the diametrical opposite of the foursquare 'service music' which, in spite of the influence of Parry and Stanford, was still the staple diet of most ecclesiastical choirs in their lifetimes. Performers should therefore seek a flexible style, in which rhythmic and dynamic inflection is rooted in the text; no bar should feel as though it is simply an iteration of the *tactus*.

New College Choir has recorded the *Songs of Farewell*, together with motets by Mendelssohn and further works by Parry, on the Novum label: *Parry: Songs of Farewell and Other Choral Works* (NCR 1394).

Songs of Farewell

Henry Vaughan
(1622–95)

C. HUBERT H. PARRY
(1848–1918)
edited by Robert Quinney

1. My soul, there is a country

Duration: *c.*32 mins

Printed in Great Britain

OXFORD UNIVERSITY PRESS, MUSIC DEPARTMENT, GREAT CLARENDON STREET, OXFORD OX2 6DP

poco rit.

stars, where stands a wing - ed sen - try, A sen - try, All skil - ful in the wars.

stars, where stands a wing-ed sen - try, All skil - - ful in the wars.

stars, where stands a wing - ed sen - try, All skil - ful, all skil - ful in the wars.

stars, where stands a wing - ed sen - try, All skil - - ful in the wars.

poco rit.

Daintily

_p_

There, a - bove noise and dan - - ger, Sweet Peace sits crowned with

There, a - bove noise and dan - - ger, Sweet Peace sits crowned with

There, a - bove noise and dan - - ger, Sweet Peace sits crowned with

There, a - bove noise and dan - - ger, Sweet Peace sits crowned with

Daintily

_p_

2. I know my soul hath power to know all things

John Davies
(1569–1626)

3. Never weather-beaten sail

Thomas Campion
(1567–1620)

4. There is an old belief

John Gibson Lockhart
(1794–1854)

Poco animando

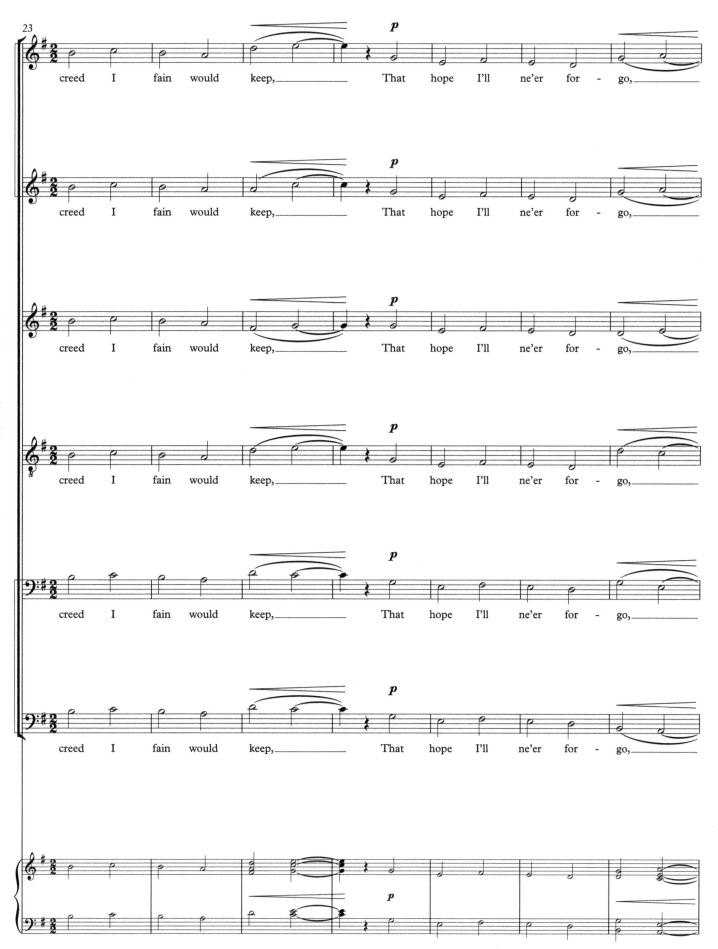

Tempo

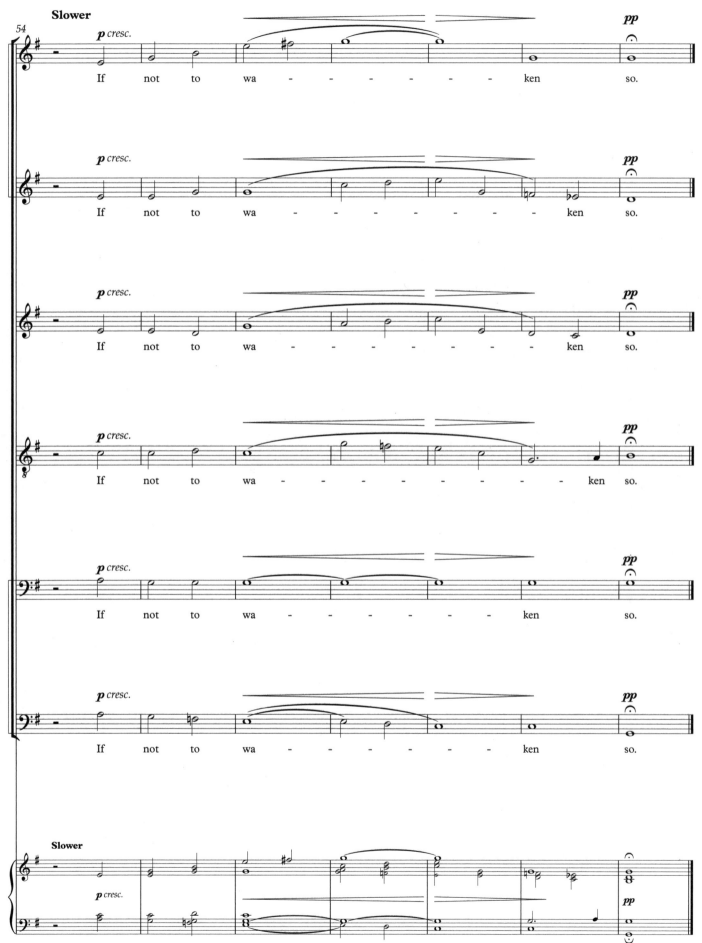

5. At the round earth's imagined corners

John Donne
(1572–1631)

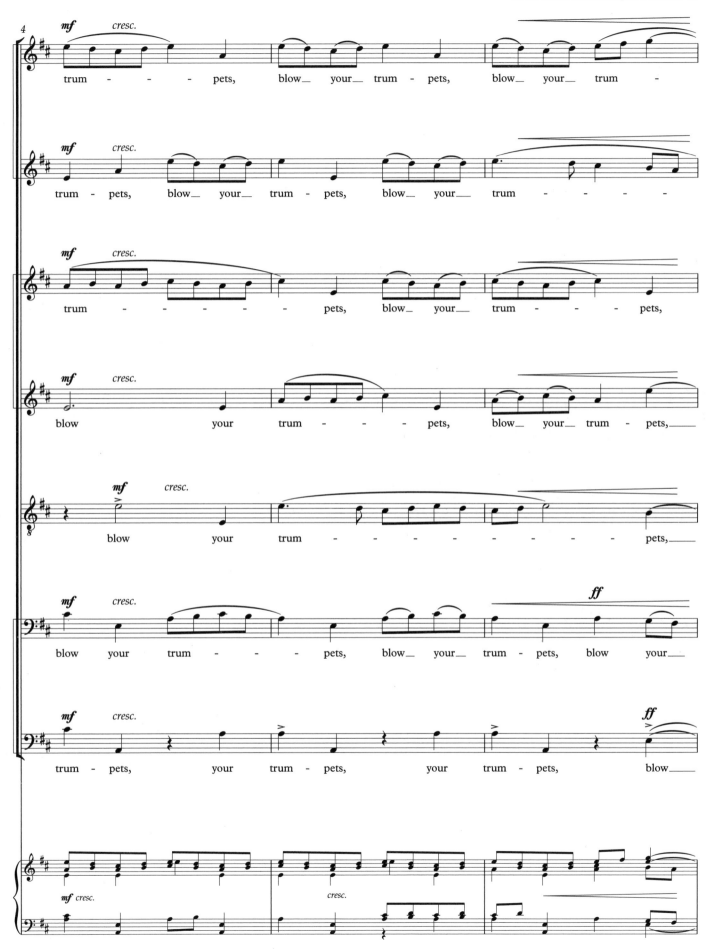

54

Poco animando

89

6. Lord, let me know mine end

Psalm 39, verses 5–15

span long; And mine age is as no-thing,

span long; And mine age is as no-thing,

span long; And mine age is as no-thing,

And mine age is as no-thing,

Thou hast made_ my days as it were a span long; And mine age is as

Thou hast made_ my days as it were a span long; And mine age is as

Thou hast made my days as it were a span long; And mine age is as

Thou hast made my days as it were a span long; And mine age is as